S POTLIGHTS

THE VIKINGS

Written by Neil Grant

OXFORD UNIVERSITY PRESS

ACKNOWLEDGMENTS

Illustrated by
Julian Baker, Chris Forcey, Steve Longden, Roger Payne, Tony Smith, Clive
Spong, Andrew Wheatcroft

Picture credits
Front cover: Top – Detail from 19th-century watercolor *Swords found at
Kilmainham-Islandbridge*; National Museum, Copenhagen. **Bottom right** –
Bishop's crozier from Thingvellir; National Museum of Iceland.

Edited by Louisa Somerville
Designed by Tony Truscott

Published in 1998 by
Oxford University Press
198 Madison Avenue
New York, New York 10016

Devised and produced by
Andromeda Oxford Limited
11-15 The Vineyard
Abingdon
Oxfordshire OX14 3PX
England

Copyright © 1998 Andromeda Oxford Limited

Library of Congress Cataloging-in-Publication Data
Grant, Neil.
        The Vikings/written by Neil Grant.
            p.   cm. — (Spotlights)
        Includes index.
        1. Vikings—Juvenile literature.   [1. Vikings.]   I. Title.
        II. Series.
DL 65. G65   1988
948'.022—dc21   97-38863
                                                               CIP
                                                                AC

ISBN 0-19-521393-9
Printed in Italy by Vallardi, Milan

CONTENTS

INTRODUCTION

More than 1,000 years ago, the Vikings were the most powerful people in Europe. Their homeland was Scandinavia — the countries we know as Denmark, Sweden, and Norway. From there they spread to other lands. The Vikings were terrifying bandits whose name means "pirates." They committed horrible slaughter among the people whose towns and monasteries they raided. Yet, there was more to the Vikings than violence and robbery. They were primarily farmers and landowners. One reason why they left home in such numbers was their desire for more and better farmland. Their search for more land and trade made them into great travelers and explorers.

FINDING OUT MORE

Archaeologists have uncovered many Viking settlements and found all kinds of objects in Viking graves. Many of these objects are now in museums around the world. Modern versions of Viking houses and ships have been made using knowledge gained from studying their remains.

HOW TO USE THIS BOOK

This book explores and explains the Viking world. Each double-page spread looks at a particular aspect of life in Viking times, building up a fascinating picture of how the Vikings lived.

HEADING

The subject matter of each spread is clearly identified by a heading prominently displayed in the top left-hand corner.

INTRODUCTION

Concise yet highly informative, this text introduces the reader to the topics covered in the spread. This broad coverage is complemented by more detailed exploration of particular points in the numerous captions.

SPOTLIGHTS

A series of illustrations at the bottom of each page encourages the reader to look out for objects from the Viking age in museums.

CRAFTS

The most impo[...] were wood and [...] craftsmen were e[...] both. Every settle[...] blacksmith and its[...] shop. In the towns[...] produced goods for[...] blacksmith would f[...] to make a sword bla[...] strips of plaited and[...] that was as good as t[...] made by Viking weap[...] Among other specialis[...] leather workers, who n[...] harnesses, shoes, caps, [...] tough enough to resist a[...] sword. The finest of all [...] were the jewelers and go[...] The Vikings were fond of[...] silver, and bronze orname[...] men and women wore the[...] indicated a person's wealth[...] could also be used as mone[...]

✓ LOOK OUT FOR THESE

■ BROOCH
The commonest [...] of jewelry were [...] arm rings, neckla[...] and pendants. La[...] round brooches [...] fastened with a [...] were made for [...] cloaks. Wome[...] wore oval broc[...] to fasten their [...] outer dress.

36

ILLUSTRATIONS
High-quality, full-color artwork brings the world of the Vikings to life. Each spread is packed with visual information.

DETAILED INFORMATION
From fierce warriors to the everyday life of farmers, the reader is given a wealth of information to help understand the Viking people.

INSET ARTWORKS
Subjects that help to explain particular points are shown as insets along with an explanation of their significance.

REFERENCE TAB
Each group of subjects is keyed with a special color to the contents page of the book so that different sections can be found quickly and easily.

BLACKSMITH
There was a blacksmith in every settlement, although the best ironwork was done in large towns and trade centers.

COMB
To make a comb from a stag's antler, a flat section was placed between the two sides of the top of the comb. The teeth were then cut with a saw, and finally the comb was decorated.

TOOLS AND WEAPONS
Iron was a precious metal to the Vikings. Nearly all their best tools and weapons were made from iron.

CARPENTER
Apart from iron, Viking craftsmen worked mainly in wood. Their ships and houses were made from wood, and they also made skillful, complicated carvings.

CARVED WOOD
Scandinavia had large forests and all men carried knives, so carving wood was common among the Vikings. Furniture and walls were decorated with carved designs such as this one.

GLASS BEADS
The Vikings did not make glass themselves, but they imported glass sticks of different colors from Germany and melted them down to make beads and other items.

WEATHER VANE
This fine weather vane of gilded bronze was once attached to a Viking ship and was later placed on a church. Now it is in a museum in Oslo, Norway.

CLAY MOLD
Bronze ornaments were cast in a clay mold. When cool, the mold was broken and the bronze removed. The ornament might then be gilded (coated with gold).

*ials
*iking
*ers in
*s own
*nter's
*s
*dern
*ult
*n)
s.

THE VIKING WORLD

From their homeland in Scandinavia, the Vikings traveled across half the world. In the east, they crossed Russia and went as far as Baghdad and Constantinople. In the west, they sailed to Iceland, Greenland, and North America, which they reached 500 years before the famous voyage made by Christopher Columbus in 1492. They founded a new nation in Iceland. They settled in Britain, Ireland, and France and had colonies in Russia. In all these places, their influence can still be seen today.

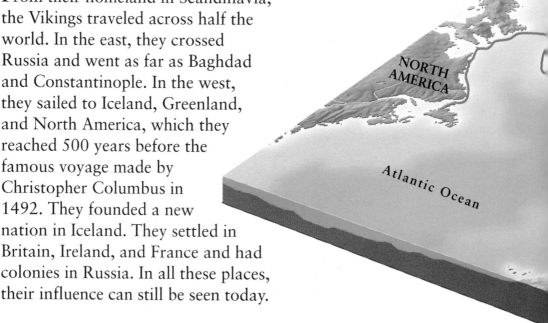

NORTH AMERICA

Atlantic Ocean

SETTLEMENTS

The main Viking settlements were in Denmark, southern Norway, and around the coasts and islands of the Baltic Sea. Trelleborg was a royal fortress, built in the 10th century, possibly by King Harald Bluetooth. The main buildings were protected by a circular earthen rampart.

NORWAY

Baltic Sea

• Trelleborg

DENMARK

LOOK OUT FOR THESE

PENDANT

The small silver pendant shown here was found in Sweden. It shows the head of a Viking and would have been worn around the neck on a chain.

FIGUREHEAD

This figurehead was found with the remains of a Viking ship. Because several well-preserved Viking ships have been found, it has been possible to make modern versions, or replicas, of them and to sail these across the North Atlantic following the original Viking routes.

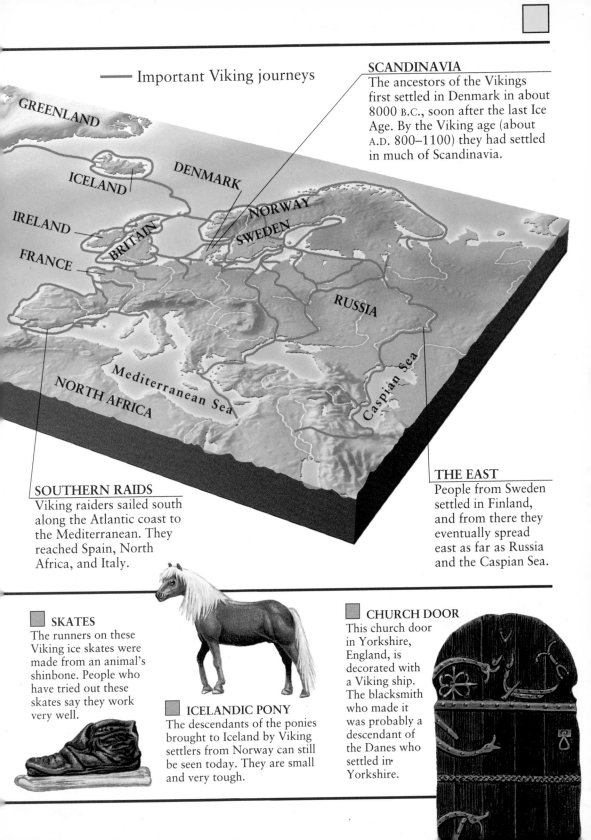

— Important Viking journeys

GREENLAND

ICELAND

IRELAND

BRITAIN

FRANCE

DENMARK

NORWAY

SWEDEN

RUSSIA

Mediterranean Sea

Caspian Sea

NORTH AFRICA

SCANDINAVIA
The ancestors of the Vikings first settled in Denmark in about 8000 B.C., soon after the last Ice Age. By the Viking age (about A.D. 800–1100) they had settled in much of Scandinavia.

SOUTHERN RAIDS
Viking raiders sailed south along the Atlantic coast to the Mediterranean. They reached Spain, North Africa, and Italy.

THE EAST
People from Sweden settled in Finland, and from there they eventually spread east as far as Russia and the Caspian Sea.

SKATES
The runners on these Viking ice skates were made from an animal's shinbone. People who have tried out these skates say they work very well.

ICELANDIC PONY
The descendants of the ponies brought to Iceland by Viking settlers from Norway can still be seen today. They are small and very tough.

CHURCH DOOR
This church door in Yorkshire, England, is decorated with a Viking ship. The blacksmith who made it was probably a descendant of the Danes who settled in Yorkshire.

FARMS AND FARMERS

Although we think of the Vikings as seagoing people, their main occupation was farming. Nearly everything they needed had to be produced on the farm; not only food, but also clothes, furniture, tools, and weapons. In the summer enough food had to be grown to last through the long winter, and if harvests were poor, people sometimes starved. A large farm like this was owned by a local chieftain. Besides his family, he had thralls (slaves) and karls (free men who did not own their own land) to help with the work. Smaller farms were sometimes grouped in villages, especially in Denmark. In Norway there were few large areas of good land, and farms were often isolated. To visit the nearest neighbor might take a day's journey, and the easiest way was by boat.

OUTBUILDINGS
Separate buildings contained a bakery, sometimes a brewery, a blacksmith's workshop, and barns for storage. Every few years the farm was abandoned and another built close by.

LOOK OUT FOR THESE

FARM CART
This piece of tapestry shows a horse-drawn wagon, used to carry people. Carts were also used on farms to carry hay and wood.

FARM TOOLS
Farmers used iron tools. Sickle blades, shown at top, were used for harvesting and have been found in many graves. Plows, shown at bottom, had an iron plowshare, or cutting blade, shown at center.

ANIMALS
Animals were allowed to wander in and out of their stables.

CROPS
Farmers grew cereals such as oats, barley, and rye, but not much wheat, except in Denmark.

FARMERS
Nearly all Vikings were farmers, even if they were also hunters, raiders, or fishermen. In flat, fertile Denmark, farming was easy. In mountainous Norway, good land was scarce.

HUNTING
Fish and other sea creatures were important foods. Fish spears like this one were made from iron and wood; fish hooks were made from bone or iron.

QUERN STONE
On most farms, grain was ground into flour with a quern, or hand mill, consisting of two small, circular stones called quern stones.

IRON ORE
Iron ore was found in bogs in Scandinavia. It was smelted in a charcoal furnace.

11

RELIGION

According to the Norse religion, when people died they made a journey, in spirit, to the next world, and so they were buried with many of their possessions for use in the afterlife. The tombs of important people were placed inside ships. The ships were then buried, or sometimes set alight and cast adrift. Ordinary graves were often marked by stones laid out in the shape of a ship. Before they became Christian, the Vikings believed in the Norse gods and goddesses, who behaved like humans with superhuman powers. The gods demanded sacrifices in exchange for sending victory to warriors and good weather to farmers. The Vikings held three religious festivals, marked by feasting, each year.

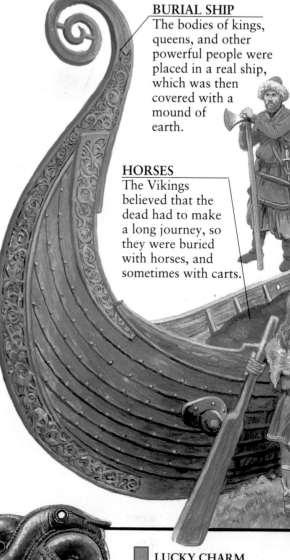

BURIAL SHIP
The bodies of kings, queens, and other powerful people were placed in a real ship, which was then covered with a mound of earth.

HORSES
The Vikings believed that the dead had to make a long journey, so they were buried with horses, and sometimes with carts.

 **LOOK OUT FOR THESE**

BRONZE THOR
Thor, the Norse god of thunder, was the most popular of the gods, especially in Norway. This small figure of Thor is made from bronze.

BROOCH
This is a brooch of the World Serpent, one of the monsters that were enemies of the gods. It lived at the bottom of the ocean. Thor once went fishing for the serpent, using a bull's head as bait.

LUCKY CHARM
The god Thor used a double-headed hammer as his weapon. It caused thunder when it was thrown. This lucky charm in the shape of Thor's hammer was worn around the neck, just as a Christian would wear a cross.

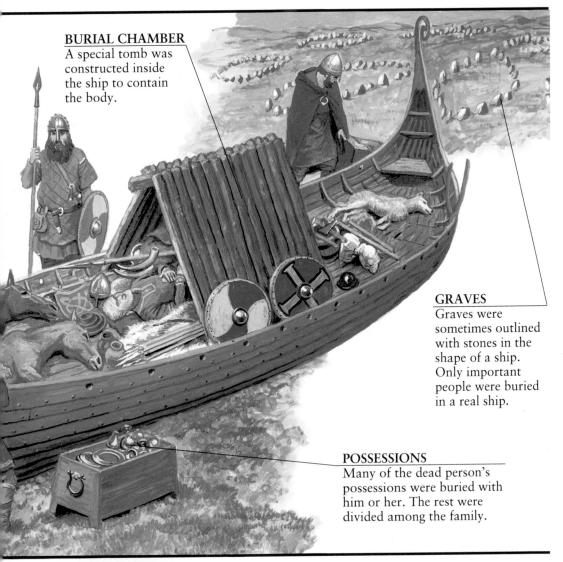

BURIAL CHAMBER
A special tomb was constructed inside the ship to contain the body.

GRAVES
Graves were sometimes outlined with stones in the shape of a ship. Only important people were buried in a real ship.

POSSESSIONS
Many of the dead person's possessions were buried with him or her. The rest were divided among the family.

RAVEN
The messenger of the mysterious, one-eyed Odin, chief of the Viking gods, was a raven. Ravens perched on Odin's shoulder and told him what was happening in the rest of the world.

STRAW ANIMAL
Straw animals were a symbol of the harvest. They were made in Viking times and are still made today.

PICTURE-STONE
The god Odin rides his eight-legged horse, Sleipnir, on this picture-stone.

VIKING RAIDS

The Vikings first appeared in other parts of northern Europe as violent raiders. They came across the sea without warning in their fast warships to attack undefended ports or island abbeys. They killed unarmed people without mercy, carried young men and women away to sell as slaves, and seized anything valuable they could find. Sometimes the Vikings sailed far up rivers to attack inland cities. In 845, more than 100 Viking ships sailed up the Seine River and attacked Paris. The king of the Franks had to pay 6,600 pounds (3,000 kilograms) of silver to make them leave.

MONASTERIES
Monks often built their monasteries on islands off the coast, where they thought they would be safe. They expected to be attacked from the land, not from the sea.

LOOK OUT FOR THESE

CARVED STONE
This stone, showing Viking warriors, was found on the island of Lindisfarne off the English coast. The abbey of Lindisfarne was one of the first places in England to suffer a Viking raid, in 793. Perhaps someone carved this stone as a record.

CASKET
This jeweled casket was found in Denmark, but it came originally from a church or abbey in Ireland, where it would have held relics of a Christian saint. It was probably stolen during a Viking raid.

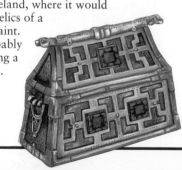

SLAVES
Besides treasure, the raiders took away young men and women to be sold as slaves.

VIKING SHIPS
Viking ships lay shallow in the water and could be driven straight onto a beach. People had little warning of their approach.

THE RAIDERS
The English called the Vikings who raided their coast "Danes," but they included Norwegians and Swedes.

TOWER
The Irish built tall bell towers like this one to give warning of Viking attacks and to provide a place of shelter.

BROOCH
This Viking brooch was made from a gold mount taken from a holy book stolen in Britain or Ireland.

SKULL
The hole in this skull of a Viking shows that the man died from a violent blow to the head, perhaps from an ax.

15

SHIPS AND NAVIGATION

The Vikings were the best seamen of their time, and their ships were the best the world had ever seen. Their long, narrow warships were light, flexible, and very seaworthy even in stormy seas, and they could sail in shallow water. They were made of oak — or pine in Norway. The wood for the curved parts was made from timber with a natural curve, so wood was never cut across the grain (which can make it split). Powered by a square sail and oars, warships could travel at 10 knots or more (nearly 12 miles, or 20 kilometers, per hour). Like other sailors, the Vikings preferred to sail close to land, but they were not afraid to cross open seas. In fact, they crossed the North Atlantic — one of the world's stormiest seas.

SAIL
Ships had a single, square sail made from strips of woolen cloth. Warships relied mainly on their oars, except on the open sea. The sail could be rolled up and the mast lowered.

STURDY FRAME
The ship's backbone, the keel, was made from a single piece of wood, to which the curved ends and the rest of the ship were added.

✓ LOOK OUT FOR THESE

■ TOOLS
Tools used by Viking shipbuilders for shaping wood and hammering nails were similar to those used by carpenters today.

■ FERRY BOAT
This boat was probably used as a ferry, to carry people and goods across a river. It was pushed along by a pole.

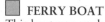

SMALL BOAT
Boats like modern rowboats were used for local travel, especially in Norway and eastern Sweden, where overland travel was hard.

OARS
Warships had 12 or more pairs of oars running the full length of the ship.

SHIELDS
Shields were mounted on the gunwale to protect the rowers from enemy weapons.

◾ STEERING BOARD
The rudder had not yet been invented, and ships were steered with a steering board (from which the word *star-board* is derived).

◾ SUN COMPASS
The Vikings had no charts or instruments, but they may have had a "sun compass." It measured the height of the sun above the horizon. From that measurement it was possible to calculate latitude (the distance from north to south).

◾ ANCHOR
Viking anchors were made from iron and looked like the anchors used today. If they could, sailors would come ashore at night to make camp on land.

WAR AND CONQUEST

Besides treasure and slaves, which could be sold, the Vikings wanted land. At first, their raids lasted a few days or weeks in summer, but soon armies began to arrive and stay all winter. Viking armies conquered all the kingdoms of Anglo-Saxon England. In 878, King Alfred of Wessex came to an agreement with the Viking leader, Guthrum, allowing the Vikings to settle in northwest England, in the region called the Danelaw. In France, Vikings led by Rollo were given Normandy by the French king in 911 or 912. Once they settled down, they defended the country against raids by other Vikings.

BAPTISM
In Alfred and Guthrum's pact, the Danes agreed to be baptized as Christians. This was a sign of peace rather than a religious conversion.

FIERCE FIGHTERS
The Vikings were fierce fighters. They had no special battle plan. It was an all-out fight of man against man.

LOOK OUT FOR THESE

WEAPONS
Double-edged swords were the chief Viking weapons. Other weapons included spears for throwing and stabbing, battle axes, and bows and arrows. Some weapons, especially swords, were richly made, with gold and silver hilts.

HELMET
The best helmets were made from iron. They had a noseguard and sometimes guards around the eyes. They never had horns.

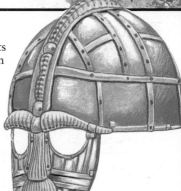

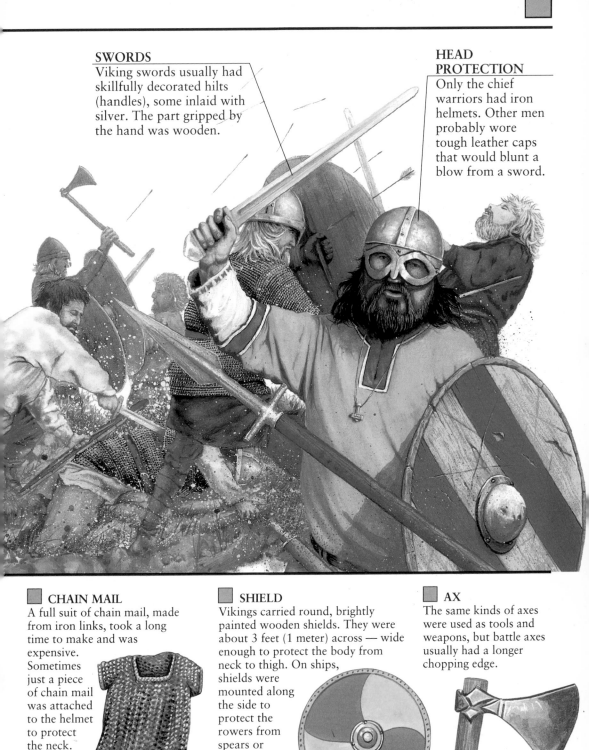

SWORDS
Viking swords usually had skillfully decorated hilts (handles), some inlaid with silver. The part gripped by the hand was wooden.

HEAD PROTECTION
Only the chief warriors had iron helmets. Other men probably wore tough leather caps that would blunt a blow from a sword.

■ **CHAIN MAIL**
A full suit of chain mail, made from iron links, took a long time to make and was expensive. Sometimes just a piece of chain mail was attached to the helmet to protect the neck.

■ **SHIELD**
Vikings carried round, brightly painted wooden shields. They were about 3 feet (1 meter) across — wide enough to protect the body from neck to thigh. On ships, shields were mounted along the side to protect the rowers from spears or arrows.

■ **AX**
The same kinds of axes were used as tools and weapons, but battle axes usually had a longer chopping edge.

SETTLEMENT

The Vikings settled in many countries beyond Scandinavia. Some of these countries, such as Britain, Ireland, and France, were inhabited, and the Vikings had to fight for their settlements. Others, such as the Faroe Islands and Iceland, were uninhabited. The settlements were led by aristocratic leaders called jarls (earls), who became independent rulers themselves, though most of their lands were taken over by kings in later times. Some of their settlements developed into important cities. Dublin, the capital of Ireland, was founded by the Vikings as a naval base in 843. It grew into a real town. Vikings also founded the independent kingdom of Man. The Isle of Man still has its own parliament.

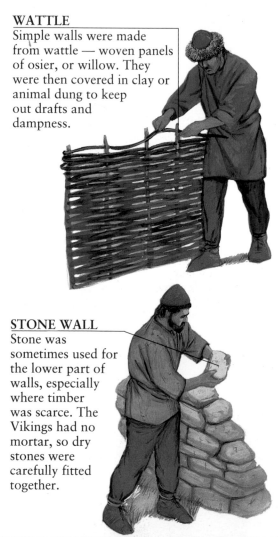

WATTLE
Simple walls were made from wattle — woven panels of osier, or willow. They were then covered in clay or animal dung to keep out drafts and dampness.

STONE WALL
Stone was sometimes used for the lower part of walls, especially where timber was scarce. The Vikings had no mortar, so dry stones were carefully fitted together.

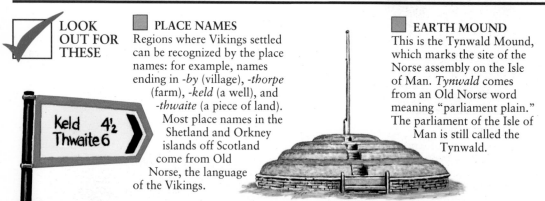

LOOK OUT FOR THESE

PLACE NAMES
Regions where Vikings settled can be recognized by the place names: for example, names ending in -by (village), -thorpe (farm), -keld (a well), and -thwaite (a piece of land). Most place names in the Shetland and Orkney islands off Scotland come from Old Norse, the language of the Vikings.

Keld 4½
Thwaite 6

EARTH MOUND
This is the Tynwald Mound, which marks the site of the Norse assembly on the Isle of Man. *Tynwald* comes from an Old Norse word meaning "parliament plain." The parliament of the Isle of Man is still called the Tynwald.

THATCH ROOF
In regions where
suitable reeds grew,
the roofs of houses
were covered in thatch.

IRELAND
The Vikings in Ireland built many
settlements for trade around the coasts.
In time, these settlements developed into
large towns, of which Dublin was the
biggest. Many of
Ireland's present-
day cities have a
Viking past.

IRELAND

Dublin •
Wicklow •
Limerick •
Wexford •
Waterford •
Cork •

ROADS
Pathways made of strong timber
were laid in towns where traffic
was heavy. Wattle panels were also
used but were unsuitable for carts.

ENGLISH HEADSTONE
This type of gravestone is found only in England.
It may be a copy of a casket, like the one on page
14. No one knows what the bears signify.

GRAVESTONE
This gravestone was found in St. Paul's Cathedral,
in London. The inscription says the stone was laid
by "Ginna and Toki," probably for someone who
died in the time of the Danish king Cnut.

TRADE

Some Vikings became very wealthy, not through booty seized in raids but through honest trade. Objects found in graves come from most parts of Europe and even Asia. Although some may be stolen goods, many were obtained through trade. In the early years, most trade took the form of barter — exchanging one kind of goods for another. But as time went on and the Vikings grew richer, more and more goods were bought and sold for money. Possibly the most valuable Viking exports were slaves and furs. Norway provided much of the fur trade and also exported timber, but it had to import grain, which could not easily be grown in the far north. Other imports included wine, salt, cloth, pottery, and glass.

SLAVES
Slaves were among the Vikings most valuable exports. They were prisoners captured in Viking raids.

LOOK OUT FOR THESE

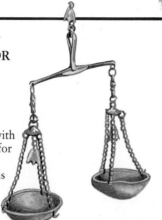

SCALES
Scales made from bronze were used with small lead weights for weighing silver. A merchant carried his scales folded up in a small box.

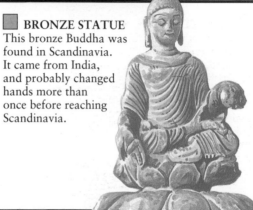

BRONZE STATUE
This bronze Buddha was found in Scandinavia. It came from India, and probably changed hands more than once before reaching Scandinavia.

TRADERS

Traders from many parts of Europe and even the Middle East visited Scandinavian trade centers.

WINE

The Vikings could not grow grapes because the climate was too cold. They imported wine from Germany and France.

TRADING ROUTES

This map shows the main trade routes of the Vikings across Europe.

SHIPS

Merchant ships were broader and deeper than warships. Some could carry 40 or 50 tons of cargo. They had a smaller crew and therefore depended mainly on sail, using oars only when necessary.

◼ CARVED ANIMALS

Amber from the Baltic, jet from northeast England, and crystal (a glasslike stone) could all be found in the Viking regions. This Viking ornament is made from jet.

◼ COINS

Coins were valued not by their type but by their weight. If the price of something was the weight of one and one-half silver coins, the buyer had to cut one coin in half.

◼ IVORY

Ivory carvings were made from walrus tusks exported from Greenland, Norway, and Iceland.

TOWNS

The Vikings were not townspeople by preference, but towns always grow up where merchants gather to do business. This is Hedeby, formerly in southern Denmark (now in Germany), which was founded before 800 and covered an area of up to 59 acres (24 hectares). All that can be seen today is the defensive rampart built in the 10th century, but archaeologists have uncovered part of the town, giving a good idea of what it looked like. Besides being a center of trade between eastern and western Europe, it also contained workshops, which may have made goods to be traded for food with nearby villages. Even a settlement as large as Hedeby was not a true town as we know it. There were no public buildings or schools, but there was a kind of town council.

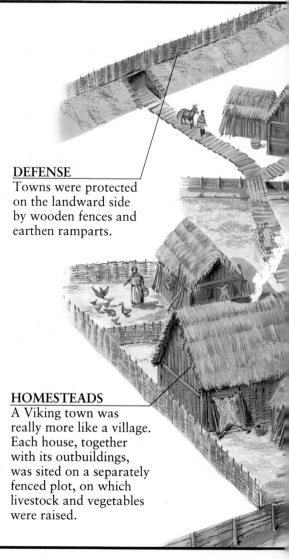

DEFENSE
Towns were protected on the landward side by wooden fences and earthen ramparts.

HOMESTEADS
A Viking town was really more like a village. Each house, together with its outbuildings, was sited on a separately fenced plot, on which livestock and vegetables were raised.

LOOK OUT FOR THESE

COMB
This comb and its case, made of horn, were intended for local trade.

CLOAK PIN
This type of pin fastened a man's cloak at his left shoulder. This one was found in Denmark and is decorated with human faces.

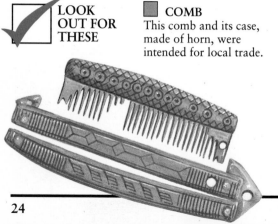

IN HARBOR

When ships were not in use, their sails were lowered and the oars stacked in Y-shaped supports on board.

WATERWAYS

Towns were usually built near the sea or on a river with access to the sea. Boats provided the easiest form of transport.

TOWNSPEOPLE

People settled in the Viking towns and traded goods with other nearby villages.

RUSHES

Rushes were sometimes put on the earthen floors of houses. When they grew dirty, the rushes were thrown out and replaced with fresh ones.

HONEY

The Vikings did not have sugar and used honey as a sweetener instead. Honey was also the main ingredient of an alcoholic drink called mead.

WELL

A town's fresh drinking water was usually drawn from a well.

THE VIKINGS IN THE EAST

Swedish merchants traveled across the Baltic Sea to Russia in the 9th century and traded with the Slav people. They traveled by boat down the great Russian rivers. When stopped by rapids, they carried their boats around them. The Dnieper River took them to the Black Sea and to Constantinople (now Istanbul), and the Volga took them to the Caspian Sea and, traveling overland by camel, to Baghdad (now the capital of Iraq). In the eastern markets they were able to buy valuable luxuries, such as silks and spices. The Swedes played a part in the growth of the city of Novgorod, their chief trading center, and in the early development of Russia.

RAPIDS
The Swedish adventurers who crossed northern Europe followed the rivers using boats. When stopped by rapids, they carried the boats around them.

LOOK OUT FOR THESE

SLEDGE
The Vikings used wooden sledges similar to modern ones for transporting goods across snow. In cold weather sledges were more useful than carts, which could get stuck in mud.

AMULET
This Arab amulet, or lucky charm, was found in Scandinavia. It may have been bought in Baghdad.

HARNESS
Harnesses for horses included saddles, bridles, bits, stirrups such as this one, and spurs.

WEAPONS
Swedish traders in Russia needed weapons to fight the Slavic tribes, who did not always welcome them.

PACKHORSES
When traveling overland, merchants used packhorses to carry their goods.

RIVERS
Rivers provided the best highways for long-distance travel. It was possible to go from the Baltic all the way to the Black Sea with only a short distance over land.

 **RUNE STONE**
Merchants who traveled to the East sometimes erected rune stones (see page 38), which recorded their travels.

HORSE COLLAR
Horses were used to pull carts, plows, and sledges. The reins passed through a horse collar, which was often beautifully made.

THE VIKINGS IN ICELAND

Vikings from Norway began to settle in Iceland in the 870s. The first settlers were led by chiefs who wanted more land or hoped to escape the growing power of the king in Norway. Except for a few Irish monks, who soon left, no one lived in Iceland before the Vikings. They created a new nation, which has lasted to the present. Unlike any other country, Viking Iceland was a kind of republic. There was no king. Laws were passed by a national assembly, the Althing — sometimes called the world's first parliament — which met at Thingvellir. It had an elected president. He had to know all the laws by heart, as they were not written down until 1119. The Althing was also a place for exchanging news and goods.

THINGVELLIR
The "Law Speaker," who was an elected judge, addressed fellow chiefs from the Law Rock, part of some lava cliffs formed long ago after a volcanic eruption.

LOOK OUT FOR THESE

HOT SPRING
Iceland has many hot springs. People who built houses close to a hot spring enjoyed hot baths even in midwinter.

FARMHOUSE
The upper walls and roof of an Icelandic farmhouse were made of turf. Turf was warmer than wood, which was scarce (although more trees grew in Iceland during Viking times).

LOCAL CHIEFS

The law and government was the business of local chiefs. Disputes were solved — usually — by discussion and a vote.

BENCHES

Men attending a *thing*, or local assembly, sat in a circle on temporary benches, made by placing boards on stone supports.

ALTHING CHIEFS

If fierce arguments seemed likely, the chiefs at the Althing left their weapons stacked well away from the meeting.

■ **SAGA**
Iceland is the home of the sagas, stories that were written down 200 or 300 years after they were first told. The sagas tell us a great deal about the Vikings and their way of life.

■ **BIRDS' EGGS**
In Viking times, huge flocks of seabirds visited the North Atlantic coasts of Iceland. Their eggs provided a welcome change of diet.

■ **BARLEY**
Although the climate was warmer than now, it was too cold in Iceland to grow wheat. Barley was grown instead and made into flat bread. Ale was brewed from malted barley.

DISCOVERERS

The best land in Iceland was soon occupied. In 985 Eric the Red led settlers from Iceland to Greenland, which he had discovered on an earlier voyage. Although most of Greenland is covered by thick ice, it has some fertile land. The grazing, fishing, and hunting were good, and the climate was not much colder than Iceland. Eric built his own homestead, and other families settled nearby. Later, they found that more land existed farther west across the ocean. Eric's son Leif reached it in about the year 1000. He found a warmer country with forests and wild grapes, and called it Vinland. Exactly where Vinland was is unknown, but the Vikings did reach North America, because remains of a settlement have been found in Newfoundland.

SALMON
Although Greenland was mostly covered in ice, nature provided plenty of food, such as salmon from the rivers.

LOOK OUT FOR THESE

SHEARS
Sheep shears such as this one were valuable tools. They would have been kept in a specially made wooden box.

HALIBUT
Greenlanders caught halibut by digging a trench in the sand at low tide. The halibut would swim in with the tide. When the tide went out again, they were trapped in the trench.

MERCHANTS

In the early years, the Greenlanders kept in touch with Iceland and Scandinavia. Merchants brought vital supplies in exchange for Greenland products such as polar-bear skins.

WINTER FOOD

Fish was hung out to dry on poles and then stored for the long winter.

VENISON

After a successful hunt for reindeer, the animals were skinned. The meat was dried and stored for the winter.

WHALEBONE

Whales provided many useful things, including meat, oil, and whalebone — the tough, bony plates from the mouths of certain whales. Whalebone could be made into many things, such as this ax head.

GRAPES

When Leif Eriksson traveled west of Greenland across the ocean, he discovered a land where wild grapes grew. He called his discovery Vinland (Wine-land). However, the exact location of Vinland remains unknown.

BUILDINGS

The Vikings built many different kinds of houses, depending on what materials were available. Their houses were not built to last very long. After some years, villages and farms were often abandoned and rebuilt nearby. Because they had open fires and no chimneys — smoke escaped through a hole in the roof — the houses often burned down. Floors were simply earth, beaten hard. Walls were lined with wood, sometimes carved into panels. Buildings had only one story, although some big farmhouses were quite tall, with wooden pillars inside to support the roof. The same kind of building might be a home, a workshop, or even (in Christian times) a church. A Viking "longhouse" often had an area at one end for storing grain or for keeping cattle in winter.

DENMARK
At Fyrkat, a royal fort in Denmark, lean-to timbers were used to support the roof.

ICELAND
Houses had thick turf walls with stone foundations and a turf roof.

IRELAND
In Dublin, outer walls were made from wattle covered in daub (mud).

DENMARK
In Aros (Århus), houses were partly sunk into the ground and had thatch roofs.

RUSSIA
In Holmgard (Novgorod), whole pine logs were used for buildings.

APPRENTICE
House building was one of the skills that every boy learned.

LOOK OUT FOR THESE

LONGHOUSE
In the Shetland Islands today there are longhouses that look like the farmhouses built by the Vikings centuries earlier. These were basically one long room with winter stables for the animals.

LAVATORY
This outside lavatory was discovered in York, England. It was a simple bench seat positioned over a large, smelly hole in the ground.

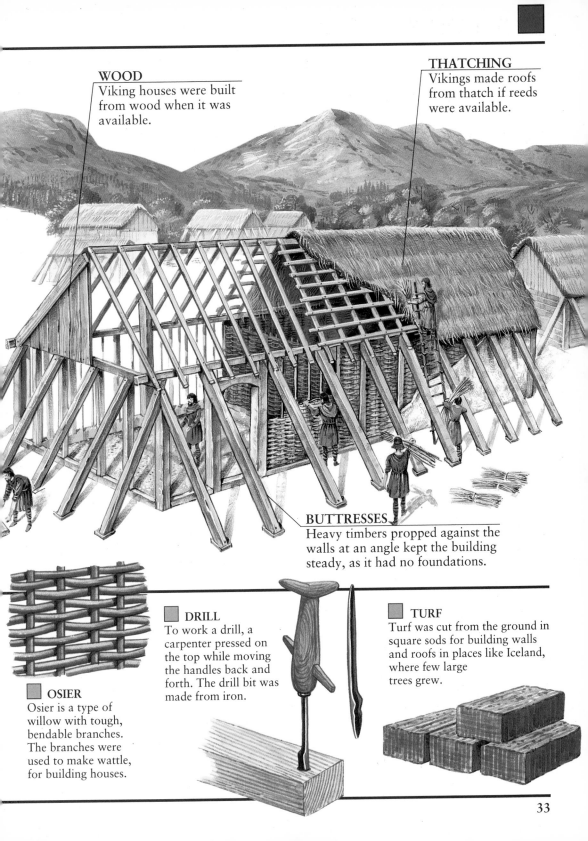

WOOD
Viking houses were built from wood when it was available.

THATCHING
Vikings made roofs from thatch if reeds were available.

BUTTRESSES
Heavy timbers propped against the walls at an angle kept the building steady, as it had no foundations.

OSIER
Osier is a type of willow with tough, bendable branches. The branches were used to make wattle, for building houses.

DRILL
To work a drill, a carpenter pressed on the top while moving the handles back and forth. The drill bit was made from iron.

TURF
Turf was cut from the ground in square sods for building walls and roofs in places like Iceland, where few large trees grew.

33

HOME LIFE

Viking homes would not seem comfortable to us. They were dark and smoky, with no windows and little furniture except for shelves, stools, and chests for clothes. The hall of a big farmstead was up to 131 feet (40 meters) long, and the sagas tell of feasts where 100 people sat down together. Benches and tables could be hauled up to the roof, out of the way, when not in use. Women were in charge of the home, and they looked after the farm when the husband was away. Although they did not have equal rights with men, they fared better than women in many other societies of the time. Children did not go to school. They helped around the farm and learned the skills they would need to survive as adults.

UTENSILS
Cooks used iron pots, bowls of soapstone or pottery, and wooden plates. People ate with a knife and spoon, or with their hands. Forks were not used.

HEARTH
In the center of the house was an open fireplace, called a hearth. It gave warmth and light, and the food was cooked here.

LOOK OUT FOR THESE

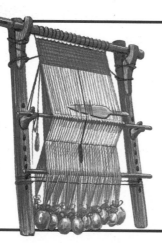

LOOM
Clothes were made at home, usually from wool. All woolens, including ships' sails, were woven on a loom such as this one.

HIGH CHAIR
The chief of the household sat on a special high chair, rather like a throne.

BOARD GAME
Board games have been found in Viking graves. One game was played with counters like checkers, but we do not know the rules.

MEAT AND VEGETABLES

Vikings ate much meat and fish, but they also grew vegetables such as cabbages and parsnips.

WOOL

Clothes were mostly made from wool. This woman is spinning yarn. A loom, for weaving the yarn into cloth, stands against the wall.

■ DRINKING HORN

Horns were made into drinking cups. The horns had no flat base on which to stand if put down.

■ MALLET

In some places linen was worn as well as wool. The stems of flax, from which linen is made, were broken down into fibers with a mallet such as this one.

■ BED

Only the rich and powerful had real wooden beds. This one belonged to a Norwegian queen who lived in the early 9th century.

CRAFTS

The most important materials were wood and iron, and Viking craftsmen were expert workers in both. Every settlement had its own blacksmith and its own carpenter's shop. In the towns, workshops produced goods for sale. A modern blacksmith would find it difficult to make a sword blade (using strips of plaited and welded iron) that was as good as the swords made by Viking weapons makers. Among other specialists were leather workers, who made harnesses, shoes, caps, and tunics tough enough to resist a slashing sword. The finest of all craftsmen were the jewelers and goldsmiths. The Vikings were fond of gold, silver, and bronze ornaments. Both men and women wore them. They indicated a person's wealth and could also be used as money.

BLACKSMITH
There was a blacksmith in every settlement, although the best ironwork was done in large towns and trade centers.

LOOK OUT FOR THESE

BROOCH
The commonest forms of jewelry were neck or arm rings, necklaces, and pendants. Large, round brooches that fastened with a pin were made for cloaks. Women wore oval brooches to fasten their outer dress.

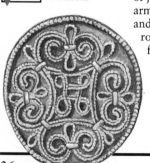

CARVED WOOD
Scandinavia had large forests and all men carried knives, so carving wood was common among the Vikings. Furniture and walls were decorated with carved designs such as this one.

COMB

To make a comb from a stag's antler, a flat section was placed between the two sides of the top of the comb. The teeth were then cut with a saw, and finally the comb was decorated.

TOOLS AND WEAPONS

Iron was a precious metal to the Vikings. Nearly all their best tools and weapons were made from iron.

CARPENTER

Apart from iron, Viking craftsmen worked mainly in wood. Their ships and houses were made from wood, and they also made skillful, complicated carvings.

■ GLASS BEADS

The Vikings did not make glass themselves, but they imported glass sticks of different colors from Germany and melted them down to make beads and other items.

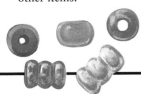

■ WEATHER VANE

This fine weather vane of gilded bronze was once attached to a Viking ship and was later placed on a church. Now it is in a museum in Oslo, Norway.

■ CLAY MOLD

Bronze ornaments were cast in a clay mold. When cool, the mold was broken and the bronze removed. The ornament might then be gilded (coated with gold).

ARTS AND POETRY

Viking art is best seen today in jewelry or carved stone. Some wood carvings have also survived, but wood and textiles, such as tapestries, usually rotted. Viking designs were lively and creative, but they were abstract, not realistic. They were based mainly on long, ribbonlike forms and strange animal heads, and even experts sometimes find them difficult to understand. Poetry was always popular among kings and nobles. Court poets were called skalds. Their poems were about heroes and battles and were learned by heart because there were no books until late in the Viking age. The Vikings had a form of writing, called runes, that was carved with a knife into wood or stone. To make them easier to cut, runes were made up of upright or slanting strokes.

RUNES
Not everyone understood runes and they were sometimes thought of as magic signs. But they were normally used for ordinary purposes, such as keeping records.

ENGRAVING
The engraved picture-stones of the Baltic island of Gotland show ships and warriors, and scenes from mythology.

LOOK OUT FOR THESE

PANPIPES
This set of wooden panpipes from Viking-age York, in England, can still be played.

BONE PIPES
Vikings enjoyed feasts and story-telling, and probably enjoyed singing, too, but we know nothing about their music. This pipe, found in Sweden, was made from an animal bone.

HARP
The Vikings had stringed instruments, including a kind of harp that may have been like the ancient harps of Celtic Britain.

STONE MEMORIALS

Most runic inscriptions that have survived today are cut in stone, but other materials, such as wood or bone, were also used.

STORYTELLER

Stories, or sagas, about famous heroes were told in early Viking times but not written down until centuries later.

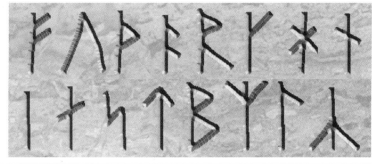

ALPHABET

Runes are difficult for people to read nowadays because the same sign may represent more than one sound — and there were no signs for some letters.

 DECORATED CUP

This little cup is decorated with two twisting, snakelike bodies with birds' heads. It came from a royal grave in Denmark.

MONUMENT

The Vikings put up stone monuments to dead relatives. Some had pictures, which were carved and then painted, as well as runic inscriptions.

KINGS AND EMPIRES

At the beginning of the Viking age, in the late 8th century, only Denmark was united under one king, and even he did not rule the whole country. Southern Norway was united by King Harold Fine-Hair in about 890. Sweden was not united until the 12th century. At this time, kings still depended on the support of nobles and chieftains. Assemblies, called *things*, made the laws. As time went on, people wanted a king who could command armies and enforce law and order over a large area. Royal government became more powerful and kings made their own laws. The greatest of them was the Danish king Cnut. Before his death in 1035, he ruled Denmark, Norway, part of Sweden, and England.

KING CNUT
Cnut's courtiers told him how great he was. "Even the tide would go out if you ordered it," they said. Cnut sat on the beach and ordered the waves to retreat. He got wet and his courtiers felt foolish!

LOOK OUT FOR THESE

RARE PICTURES
In Viking Scandinavia, pictures of real people were rare. This drawing of King Cnut and his queen is from an English manuscript.

CATHEDRAL
This is the door of St. Magnus Cathedral in Kirkwall, Orkney, built by a Norse jarl (earl) of Orkney in the 12th century. The jarls were powerful, independent princes who at one time also ruled part of Scotland, including the Western Isles.

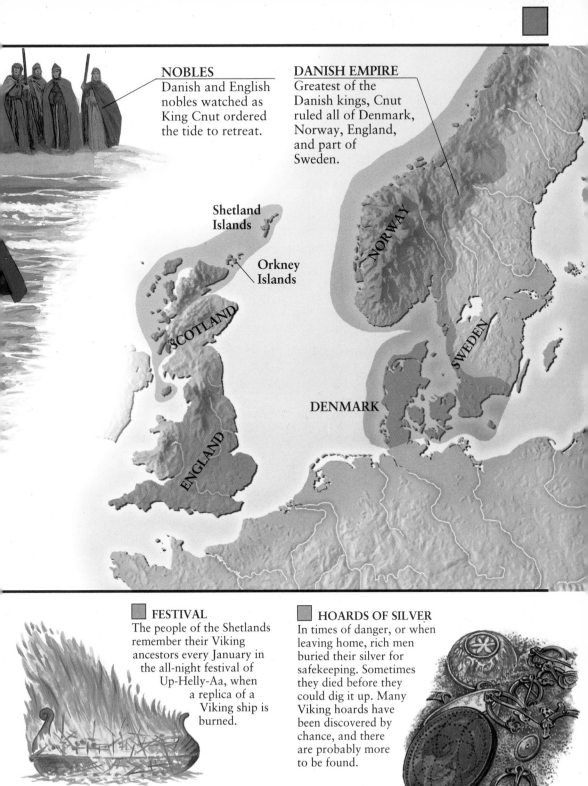

NOBLES
Danish and English nobles watched as King Cnut ordered the tide to retreat.

DANISH EMPIRE
Greatest of the Danish kings, Cnut ruled all of Denmark, Norway, England, and part of Sweden.

Shetland Islands

Orkney Islands

NORWAY

SWEDEN

SCOTLAND

DENMARK

ENGLAND

FESTIVAL
The people of the Shetlands remember their Viking ancestors every January in the all-night festival of Up-Helly-Aa, when a replica of a Viking ship is burned.

HOARDS OF SILVER
In times of danger, or when leaving home, rich men buried their silver for safekeeping. Sometimes they died before they could dig it up. Many Viking hoards have been discovered by chance, and there are probably more to be found.

THE END OF THE VIKINGS

The age of the Vikings did not end suddenly, but the defeat of King Harald Hardrada by the English king Harold Godwinson in 1066 was a sign that the age of the Vikings was over. Raiding was no longer so easy. Changes in farming methods had reduced the need for more land. In places where Vikings had settled down, they had become no different from their neighbors, and Scandinavia had become a Christian land. Although Christianity did not prevent wars, it taught that killing was wrong. One sign of this change was the large number of churches that were built in Scandinavia. Like other buildings, they were made of wood. They were built from planks, like a ship, and are known as stave churches.

DRAGON HEADS

As well as Christian crosses, the Borgund church has Viking dragon heads, to protect it from demons.

LOOK OUT FOR THESE

CASTLES

Stone castles started to be built in Europe in the 11th century. They were far too strong to be captured by old-fashioned Viking raids.

RECONSTRUCTION

In recent years we have learned much more about the Vikings through the work of archaeologists. At many sites in Scandinavia, Britain, and Ireland, Viking settlements have been reconstructed.

CARVING
Stave churches contain elaborate carved decoration. So far as we know, Viking houses had nothing like this, although it may simply be that no such carving has survived.

STAVE CHURCHES
Scandinavian Christians built magnificent wooden churches, such as this one at Borgund, Norway. The walls were made of upright timbers held by horizontal beams at top and bottom, like the staves of a barrel.

KEEPING DRY
The method of stave construction allowed the whole building to be raised above the ground, so the wood would not rot.

BAYEUX TAPESTRY
Soon after the defeat of Harald Hardrada, England was successfully invaded by the Normans. The Norman Conquest was recorded in the Bayeux Tapestry. *Norman* means "Norseman" — the first Normans were Viking settlers. However, by 1066 their descendants had become French men and women.

STONE CROSS
This stone cross shows a Viking warrior buried with his weapons in the old Viking way, although he was a Christian. Several monuments like this can be seen in northern England.

GLOSSARY

Words in SMALL CAPITAL letters indicate a cross-reference.

Althing The assembly of free men that passed laws and settled disputes in Iceland.

archaeologist A person who studies the past — especially the ancient past before people kept written records — through objects, buildings, graves, and other remains.

Bayeux Tapestry A huge embroidery that records the Norman Conquest of England in words and pictures, in a long panel like a comic strip.

booty Valuables gained by robbery or war.

casket A small chest or box in which to keep jewels and precious ornaments.

Danegeld Money paid by European rulers to VIKING raiders to make them leave their countries.

Danelaw The area of England (roughly the northeast) awarded to the VIKINGS in the late 9th century.

Daneverk A defensive RAMPART that was built across southern Denmark in VIKING times against hostile tribesmen.

fortress A strongly defended settlement, town, or castle.

gods The chief gods of the VIKINGS were ODIN and THOR, but there were many others. Stories about the gods were well known to SCANDINAVIANS from their childhood onward.

gravestone A stone marking a grave. A gravestone is usually inscribed with the name and dates of the person who has been buried.

gunwale The top edge of the side of a boat.

hilt The handle of a sword.

hoard A hidden store of treasure.

jarl The OLD NORSE word for "earl." A jarl was a local ruler who was sometimes as powerful as a king.

knorr A VIKING cargo ship.

longhouse A typical VIKING house, made up of one long room plus stables and storerooms at one end.

loom A simple machine used for weaving threads of wool into cloth.

mead An alcoholic drink made with honey.

merchant A person who made a living from buying and selling goods. In VIKING times, merchants traveled to markets in distant countries.

monastery A place where MONKS live.

monk A man who has devoted his life to God.

Norseman Another name for a VIKING.

Odin One of the chief VIKING GODS, and the god of war. He was also a magician who could change his shape when he wanted, and he could see into the future.

Old Norse The language spoken by the VIKINGS, from which modern SCANDINAVIAN languages developed.

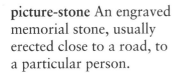

picture-stone An engraved memorial stone, usually erected close to a road, to a particular person.

plow A farming tool with sharp blades for turning over the earth before seed is sown. A plow is attached to an animal such as a horse or an ox, or — in richer countries nowadays — a tractor.

rampart A long mound made of earth, built as a form of defense, often with a fence on top.

runes Signs used for writing, like the letters in a modern alphabet. They were carved into wood or stone slabs.

saga A story of events, heroes, and famous families in Iceland and Norway during VIKING times. At first sagas were told by word of mouth. They were first written down in the 12th century.

Scandinavia The VIKING lands of Norway, Sweden, Denmark, Iceland, and Finland.

sickle A curved blade with a short handle, used for cutting grass or corn.

skald A poet who entertained the households of chiefs and royalty. A skald recited long poems about the bravery of warriors and kings.

slave A person who was owned and could be bought or sold, like a piece of property. A slave had no rights.

Slavs The people who live in much of eastern Europe.

soapstone A soft rock, which is easily carved, found mainly in Norway. The VIKINGS made bowls and dishes from soapstone.

sod A square piece of TURF cut from grassy land. Sod was used for building houses.

starboard The right-hand side of a ship or boat. Its name is taken from the STEERING BOARD.

steering board A wooden paddle attached to the side of a ship and used for steering in the days before the rudder was invented.

Thor The VIKING GOD of storms, thunder, and strength. He was believed to ride across the sky in a chariot that created storms.

thrall OLD NORSE word for a SLAVE.

turf Slabs of earth used in house building.

Viking A fighter at sea or a pirate. In Viking times, people used other names for the Vikings, such as Danes or NORSEMEN (meaning "North men").

wattle and daub A mixture of twigs, straw, animal hair, and clay used for making fences or walls. The wattles (twigs) are woven into a framework and covered in clay (daub).

weather vane A flat piece of metal or other material, often arrow-shaped, placed on top of a mast or church spire. It rests on a pivot, which allows it to turn, showing which way the wind is blowing.

INDEX